ENDLESS PATH

Greek Myth

This is a **FLAME TREE** book
First published in 2007

Publisher and Creative Director: Nick Wells
Editor: Catherine Emslie
Designer: Mike Spender
Picture Researcher: Gemma Walters
Production: Chris Herbert and Claire Walker

Special thanks to: Rosanna Singler

FLAME TREE PUBLISHING
Crabtree Hall, Crabtree Lane
Fulham, London SW6 6TY
United Kingdom
www.flametreepublishing.com

07 09 11 10 08
1 3 5 7 9 10 8 6 4 2

Flame Tree is part of The Foundry Creative Media Company Limited
Copyright © The Foundry 2007

All rights reserved. No part of this publication may be reproduced, stored in a retrieval
system or transmitted in any form or by any means, electronic, mechanical,
photocopying, recording or otherwise, without the prior permission of the publisher.

A copy of the CIP data for this book is available from the British Library.

ISBN 978 1 84451 735 X

Every effort has been made to contact copyright holders. In the event of an oversight
the publishers would be glad to rectify any omissions in future editions of this book.

Printed in China

ENDLESS PATH

Greek Myth

Author: Rachel Storm

Consultant: Dr Stephen Instone

FLAME TREE
PUBLISHING

Contents

Foreword

One of the attractions of Greek mythology is its duality of readership, its appeal both to children for the myths' entertainment value and to adults who can read more into them. Odysseus' encounter with Polyphemus, for example, reveals on the one hand the hero overcoming adversity, on the other the Greeks' concern with identifying civilization in contrast to what is non-Greek. We can see the same double-pull in the writings of modern authors such as J.K. Rowling, Philip Pullman and Melvin Burgess, the first two's books in fact being available with different covers for children and adults.

Heroes and gods co-exist in Greek myth. In some respects the gods represent personifications of natural forces, and so for the Greeks they could provide explanations of abnormal or superhuman behaviour – for example, Perseus is helped by Athena and that explains his superhuman abilities. Similarly, the Greeks believed that a victor in the ancient Olympic Games owed his almost superhuman achievement to the help of the gods. But the Greeks also had an anthropomorphic conception of the gods and saw them as quasi-human, comparable to modern celebrities of iconic status such as David and Victoria Beckham to whom people look up but who are accompanied also by normal human frailties. However, in certain key areas the gods are different from mortals: they are immortal, do not grow old and do not need to work for their survival. Many Greek myths exploit this contrast: in *The Iliad*, Achilles is increasingly reminded that his glory will be shortly followed by his death, most poignantly when the goddess Hera endowers Achilles' immortal horse Rhaenus with speech and the horse prophesies to Achilles that he will soon die.

Monsters feature in many Greek myths, and they are nearly always feminine — take, for instance, Medusa, the Chimaera and Scylla. Men and women were heavily segregated in the Greek world, so there was a lack of understanding and fear of women which gave rise to the portrayal in myth of these fearsome monsters. Because a woman's place was in the home, women in myth can also represent the home to which the hero (Odysseus, Agamemnon) is drawn back. The survival of the family unit was as much an issue then as it is now.

The sources for Greek mythology include not only literature but vase-painting and sculpture. Imbibing Greek mythology was a general public experience. Some of the most famous myths were represented on Greek temples, one obvious example being the Parthenon, on which featured the contest between Poseidon and Athena for possession of Attica and the battle between the Lapiths and Centaurs. And every spring in Athens tragedies were staged enacting the myths, often interlacing them with contemporary resonances. The stories of Agamemnon, Oedipus and Medea are best known from the plays of Aeschylus, Sophocles and Euripides. Greek mythology was for everyone and in this respect has its counterpart in modern forms of media (television caters to a wide audience hungry for storytelling with both its high-brow programmes and sheer entertainment).

Greek authors exploited mythology in a number of ways. The poetess Sappho used the story of Helen to justify her own love for a girl-friend. She says that the best thing in the world is whatever one loves, and tells how Helen deserted her husband, parents and child, led on by love and Paris; similarly, Sappho loves her friend Anactoria more than anything in the world. The philosopher Plato used mythology as a means of persuading in areas where rational argument is less cogent: with a number of eschatological myths describing the horrors that await sinners in the Underworld he tried to convince his readers why they should lead a good life. Herodotus, 'the father of history', tells of one-eyed men and griffins who guard gold as he fuses myth and history in his attempt to characterize the distant peoples of Scythia. The Greek word from which 'myth' derives is *mythos* which means 'word' or 'story', and many Greek myths derive from stories passed on orally which could be freely adapted to fit new contexts.

Greek Myth is an admirable account of the main stories and characters that make up Greek mythology, while setting them in their real physical context and revealing their continuing relevance to us today. Drawing on Homer and Hesiod, as well as countless other sources, it reminds us of the importance and beauty of this unforgettable aspect of the ancient Greek world.

Shelley Instone, Roehampton University

Stephen Instone, University College London

Land, Sea and Sky: The Cradle of Myth

The Myths

Thousands of years ago an extraordinarily rich body of stories arose in a region of the Mediterranean. These stories helped people to give meaning to the world and their place within it and to bring about a sense of what it was to be Greek. As Greek power spread, so too did the stories, reaching parts of southern Italy and Sicily, coastal regions of Asia Minor and north Africa and, later still, as far as Egypt and Afghanistan. Generation after generation adopted and adapted the Greek myths which were told and retold and are still being retold today.

Sources

The Greek myths have three main
sources: Homer (8th century BC),
Hesiod (late 8th century BC) and the
Homeric Hymns (7th–5th century
BC), poems composed by writers in
the epic tradition. Homer's *Iliad* and
Odyssey and Hesiod's *Theogony*
would have been told and sung
at religious rituals, banquets
and festivals.

Later Sources

Myths were also conveyed by lyric poets, most famously Pindar, and dramatists, especially the three great 5th-century-BC Athenian tragedians – Aeschylus, Sophocles and Euripides. Later sources included Apollonius of Rhodes's *Argonautica* (3rd century BC) and, in Roman times, Ovid's *Metamorphoses* and Virgil's *Aeneid*. In addition, sculptures, murals, mosaics and vase paintings preserved scenes and characters from the great stories.

Minoans

Minoan civilization began on Crete some 5,000 years ago when the island was settled by a people who probably came from Asia Minor. The Minoans were peace-loving; their religion centred on goddess worship which took place at magnificent cult centres such as the palace at Knossos. Minoan civilization was at its height from around 1700 to about 1450 BC when it came to an abrupt end. This sudden demise was probably the result of a series of natural disasters or possibly a collapse in trade. Whatever its cause, the Minoans were overcome by the Mycenaeans who inherited their deities as well as their land.

Mycenaeans

The people we know as the Greeks were originally nomadic Indo-Europeans who entered the region from the north sometime around 1900 BC. They brought with them a pantheon of deities including a sky-god, something like Zeus, and became known as the Mycenaeans. At some point they adopted the goddesses of the older Minoan culture. They were also influenced by Near Eastern civilizations. Mycenaean culture ended quite abruptly, sometime around 1100 BC, as a consequence of invasion, natural disaster or famine. If any civilization can be said to live on, it must surely be that of the Myceaneans, who later influenced Homer's *Iliad* and *Odyssey*.

Landscape

The Sea

Virtually cut off by inhospitable mountains from the European continent, the Greeks were forced to take to the sea. From the Olympian Poseidon to the goddess Aphrodite, from nymphs to monsters, time and again the sea embodies ancient Greek preoccupations and moral thinking in splendid personalities and stories.

Mountains

Mountains were inaccessible, dangerous and
exhilarating places where mortals might
encounter the gods. Mount Olympus, the
highest mountain in Greece, was where the
Olympian gods lived and held court while the
baby Zeus was sheltered in a cave on Mount
Dikte or Mount Ida. The Titans were so large that
they used the mountains as their thrones.

Caves

To the ancient Greeks, entering a cave was like entering the womb of the earth goddess Gaia. Caves symbolized passage to the divine and also wild and untamed nature. In the story of Odysseus and the Cyclopes, for example, the giant Polyphemus lives in a cave.

Rivers and Springs

In sun-parched Greece, fresh water was of vital importance. It played a crucial
part in many religious ceremonies including sacrifices. The Greeks regarded rivers
as virile male deities, usually with horns and long beards, the sons of the Titans
Oceanus and Tethys.

'And there are as many tumbling and rushing rivers,

all sons of Okeanos and queenly Tethys.

It is hard for a mortal to recite the names of all,

but those who live by them know each of their names.'

Hesiod's *Theogony, c.* 700 BC

Places and Foundation Myths

Delphi

A city at the foot of Mount Parnassus, Delphi became famous as the centre of the world and the site of the temple to Apollo. A story tells how the great god Zeus released two eagles from opposite ends of the earth. The birds met at Delphi whereupon the place was pronounced the earth's navel (omphalos). The exact spot was marked by a large carved stone.

The Oracle

Delphi was originally called Pytho, probably after Python, the monstrous serpent or dragon said to guard the famous oracle there. Python may have been the child of the ancient earth goddess Gaia. Apollo killed the Python, an act which some have seen as the male sky god overcoming the female earth goddess, and established his own oracle at the site. He gave advice through his priestess, the Pythia, who sat on a tripod above the shrine and would respond to questions while in a trance. The original Temple to Apollo, built on the site of the oracle, dates back to the 6th century BC.

Athens

Named after the goddess Athena, Athens was a great centre of learning. According to legend, the sea god Poseidon competed with Athena to become patron of the city. Poseidon produced a salt pool but Athena won the contest by creating an olive tree. Both pool and tree were worshipped on the Acropolis (the central, raised-up district of a Greek city). Cecrops, half man half serpent, was the legendary first king of Athens. He was said to be born either from the soil, or from the earth goddess Gaia. He introduced burial and marriage rituals as well as bloodless sacrifices and taught the Athenians how to read and write.

Troy

Also known as Ilios or Ilium, Troy was the city of the legendary King Priam and Queen Hecuba. Their son Paris abducted Helen, wife of Menelaus, King of Sparta, and took her to Troy thereby sparking the legendary Trojan War. The historical site of the city was discovered in northwest Asia Minor near the coast of the Aegean in 1873 by the German archaeologist Heinrich Schliemann (1822–90). Excavations have shown that it was built and destroyed nine times. The ruins dating back to around 1250 BC are probably those of King Priam's city which was laid waste at the time by Agamemnon and his Greeks.

The Founding of Troy

Ilus was the son of Tros who was descended from Dardanus, the son of Zeus and Elektra. One day, Ilus won a wrestling contest held by the king of Phrygia. He was rewarded with fifty youths, fifty maidens and a cow. The king told Ilus to found a city wherever the cow lay down to rest. The cow lay down on the hill of Ate and there Ilus founded Ilium. Ilus prayed to Zeus whereupon the Palladium, a statue of the goddess Pallas, descended from the heavens. It shone so brightly that Ilus was blinded. Later, however, Ilus made offerings to Athena and his sight returned.

Sparta

Sparta (also known as Lacedaemon) was the capital of a region known as Laconia in the south east of the Peloponnese. It was founded by Lelex, who was born from the earth and was named after his granddaughter, a nymph. A later ruler, King Tyndareus married Leda and had many children by her including, in some accounts, Castor (one of the Dioskouroi), Clytemnestra and Helen. Tyndareus left Sparta to his son-in-law Menelaus who had married Helen. It was the abduction of Helen by Paris, prince of Troy, which sparked off the Trojan War.

Thebes

One day Zeus abducted Europa, the sister of Cadmus, whereupon her brothers went in search of her. The Delphic Oracle told Cadmus to stop worrying about his sister and instead to follow a cow and found a city where she stopped to rest. Cadmus did as told. The cow lay down to rest in Boeotia, and there he founded the city of Cadmea, later called Thebes. The city was to become one of the most important powers in ancient Greece. Amphion, son of Antiope and Zeus, later reinforced Thebes by building its marvellous seven-gated wall; he is said to have charmed the stones into place by playing his lyre.

'...the walls and towers of Thebes rose to the sound
of Amphion's lyre ...'

Euripides, *Phoenician Women*, 410 BC

Olympia

Long ago, there were five brothers known as the Dactyls. One day, they came to Olympia, a valley on the west coast of the Peloponnese peninsula. There, they ran a race against one another; the winner received an olive branch. The winner announced that, since there were five brothers, games would be held at that very same place every five years (by ancient Greek counting; every four years by modern counting). Historically, the games are first known to have been held in 776 BC as a religious festival honouring Zeus. They were banned in 394 AD when the Christian Roman emperor Theodosius I banned all pagan festivals, but were revived in the late 19th century.

The Hellespont

The Hellespont was the name the ancient Greeks gave to the Dardanelle Straits which link the Aegean Sea with the Sea of Marmara. It was named after Helle, the daughter of King Athamas and the nymph Nephele. Athamas abandoned Nephele for a mortal woman, Ino, who hated both Helle and her brother Phrixus. Secretly, Ino bribed the local oracle to say that nothing would grow unless Phrixus were sacrificed. Luckily, Nephele sent a winged golden ram to rescue the children. They climbed onto the creature's back and flew to safety. However, half way across the sea, Helle tumbled down into the waves and drowned.

Land, Sea and Sky: The Cradle of Myth

Arcadia

Named after Arcas, the son of Zeus
and the nymph Callisto, Arcadia is a
mountainous region in the centre of
the Peloponnese peninsula. It was
often represented as a paradise by
Greek and Roman poets and was
famed as the birthplace of Pan, the
god of shepherds and goatherds.

Mythical Geography

The ancient Greeks thought of themselves as living at the very centre of a disc-shaped world consisting of several concentric circles. Around the very outside of the earth ran an enormous river called Oceanus and high above towered Mount Olympus, home of the gods. The edges of the earth were where fabulous creatures and monsters lived. To the west lay seas and regions filled with monsters such as the Cyclopes and Sirens. Furthest west lay Hesperia, the blissful land of the nymphs who guarded the goddess Hera's golden apples. Hesperia has been variously placed in Arcadia, Libya , Spain and Africa.

Mapping the Unknown

Also to the far west, in the waters of Oceanus, lay the Isles of the Blessed. This was where favoured mortals, heroes or sometimes those who had simply lived good and god-fearing lives, went when they died. In the east were the barbarians, the uncivilized non-Greek-speaking races, while to the far south were the Ethiopians, a lucky, virtuous people with whom the gods banqueted. In the very north, at the edge of the world, beyond the home of the north wind Boreas, lived the Hyperboreans. They enjoyed endless sunshine and perfect happiness and could not be approached by land or sea.

The Underworld

Underworld Rivers

The underworld was thought to lie either far beyond Oceanus or way beneath the earth, connected thereto by caves and rivers. The five rivers associated with the underworld were the river of grief called Acheron, the river of wailing called Cocytus, the river of fire called Phlegethon, the river of hate called Styx and the river of forgetfulness called Lethe. Charon the boatman ferried souls to the underworld, sometimes across the River Acheron, in other accounts across the Styx. Passengers had to pay him with a coin which they carried in their mouths.

The Asphodel Fields

The gate of the underworld was guarded by Cerberus, a monstrous dog that drooled black venom. Cerberus allowed everyone to enter but no-one to leave. Accounts of the underworld varied. Most souls spent their time wandering like shadows in the Asphodel Fields, a place of neither pleasure nor pain.

Elysium and Tartarus

The exceptionally great heroes were sent to Elysium while the wicked were sent to Tartarus, a vast realm of darkness and place of punishment. Tartarus was where the Titans were confined; it lay as far beneath the earth as the earth lies beneath the heavens and was enclosed with a fence of bronze. According to some accounts, the souls that reached Elysium were able to return to earth and start a new life. Before doing so, they had to drink from the waters of the River Lethe so that they forgot everything that had gone before.

A Universal Appeal: Greek Myth Endures

'We are all Greeks. Our laws, our literature, our religion,

our arts, have their root in Greece.'

Percy Bysshe Shelley (1792–1822), 'Hellas'

The End of Myth?

In the sixth century AD, a thousand years after it had been built, the Parthenon in Athens was converted into a Christian church. The goddess Athene's temple was now dedicated to the Virgin Mary. However, the spread of Christianity did not signal the demise of the Greek myths. Instead, pagan myths were incorporated into Christian worship and culture and Christian monks laboriously copied out ancient Greek literature.

The Battle of Samson and Heracles

In the middle ages, a popular game called 'tables' (something like backgammon) was played with pieces divided into two sets; one set traditionally showed the labours of Heracles, the other showed the feats of the Old Testament hero Samson.

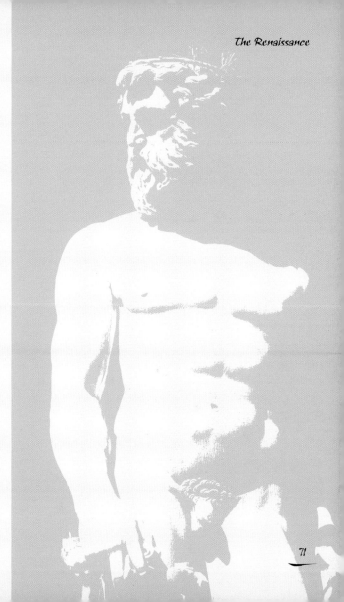

The Renaissance

The boldness and immediacy of Greek myths proved enormously inspiring to Renaissance artists. Among the period's best known paintings are Botticelli's *La Primavera* and *The Birth of Venus* as well as Titian's *Venus and Adonis*. Thousands of images of Aphrodite (known to the Romans as Venus) were executed during the period.

Renaissance Writers Influenced by the Greek Myths

Dante Alighieri (1265–1321) (*The Divine Comedy*)

William Shakespeare (1564–1616) ('Venus and Adonis',

A Midsummer Night's Dream, Troilus and Cresida)

Christopher Marlowe (1564–93) (*Dr Faustus*)

Edmund Spenser (1552/3–99) (*The Faerie Queene*)

Jean Racine (1639–99) (*Andromaque*)

Francis Bacon (1561–1626) (*The Wisdom of the Ancients*)

Dante's Odysseus

At the end of Homer's *Odyssey*, Odysseus learns that he is to make
a final voyage. It is this journey which Dante explores in Canto XXVI
of his 'Inferno', describing how Odysseus finally dies while sailing
too far out in his thirst for knowledge:

'Joyful were we, and soon it turned to weeping;

For out of the new land a whirlwind rose,

And smote upon the fore part of the ship.

Three times it made her whirl with all the waters,

At the fourth time it made the stern uplift,

And the prow downward go, as pleased Another,

Until the sea above us closed again.'

Dante, Divine Comedy, 'Inferno', Canto XXVI

Opera

With its great themes and exaggerated characters, Greek myth
has been a favourite choice for many opera composers.
A few works are listed here:

Claudio Monteverdi *La Favola d'Orfeo* (1607)

Marc-Antoine Charpentier *Medee* (1693)

George Frideric Handel *Semele* (1744)

Christoph Gluck *Orfeo ed Euridice* (1762)

Jacques Offenbach *Orpheus in the Underworld* (1858)

Richard Strauss *Elektra* (1909)

Igor Stravinsky *Oedipus Rex* (1927)

The Romantics

In the eighteenth and nineteenth centuries, Romanticism stirred up what became known as a 'cult of Greece'. New translations of Homer and the Greek tragedies inspired poems such as John Keats's 'Endymion' (1818) and Percy Bysshe Shelley's 'Prometheus Unbound' (1820). In Germany and Austria, Johann Wolfgang Goethe (1749–1832), Friedrich von Schiller (1759–1805), Friedrich Holderlin (1770–1843) and Franz Schubert (1797–1828) were all inspired by the stories of the ancient gods and heroes.

The Pre-Raphaelites

For the mid-nineteenth-century Pre-Raphaelite Brotherhood, Greek myth
provided a retreat from their newly industrialized world. Greece was
transformed into a lost paradise, a perfect world of beautiful, languid
women and splendid heroes. Edward Burne-Jones (1833–98) painted a
series of works around the Greek myth of Perseus while Hylas, Echo,
Narcissus, Circe, the Sirens, Jason and Medea, were just some of the many
characters painted by John William Waterhouse (1849–1917).

81

'Apollonian' and 'Dionysian'

The terms Apollonian and Dionysian, developed by German philosopher Friedrich Nietzsche (1844–1900), are still used as a type of shorthand for describing and understanding art, culture and individuals:

Apollonian	*Dionysian*
Reason	Passion
Order	Spontaneity
Moderation	Excess
Control	Irrationality
Culture	Intuition

Freud's Oedipus Complex

Sigmund Freud (1856–1939) believed that certain myths told stories that had an important part to play in an individual's psychological development. For example, he felt that the story of Oedipus, Jocasta and Laius summed up the growing male child's feelings of resentment towards his father and attachment to his mother. Freud called this formative stage of development the Oedipus Complex.

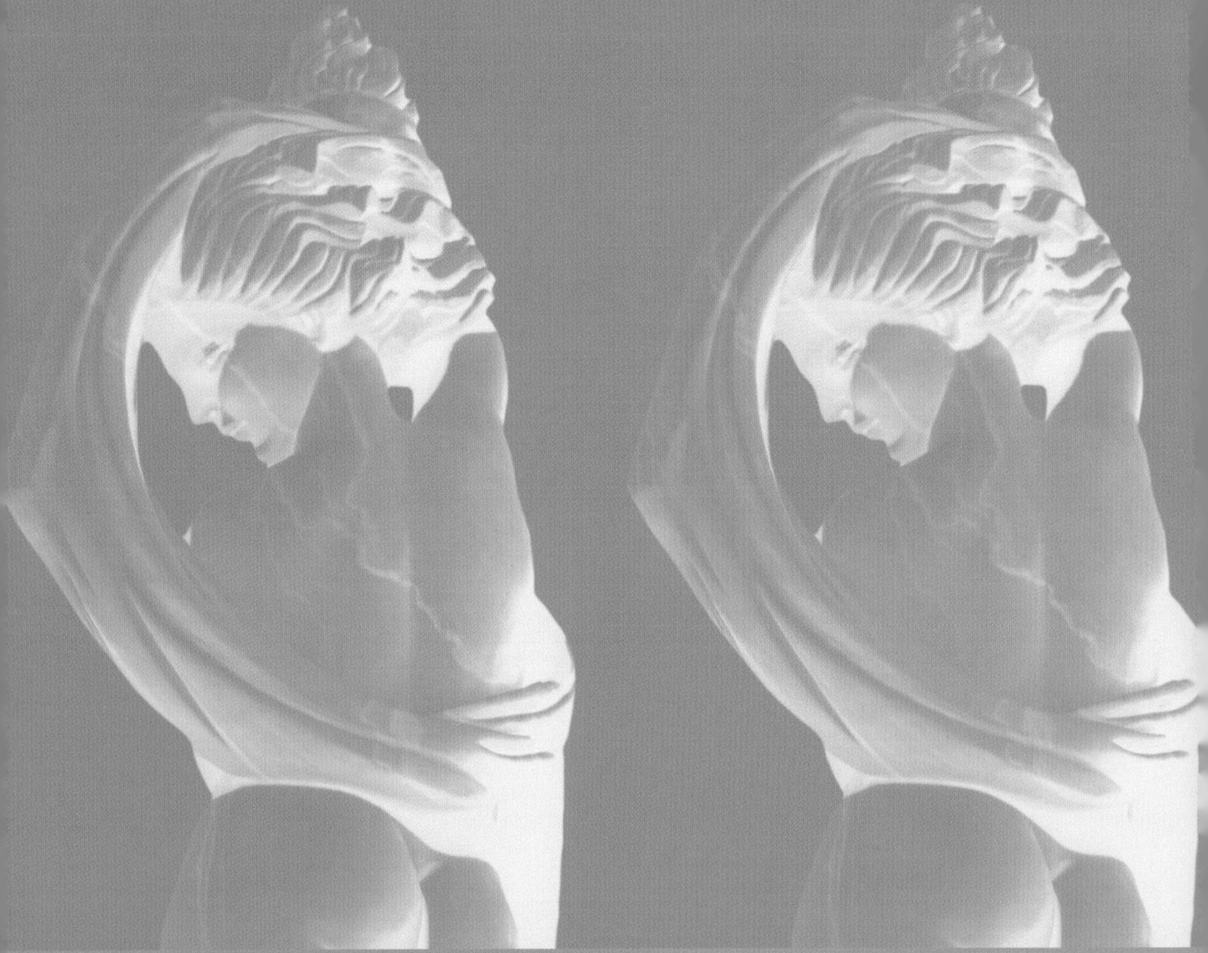

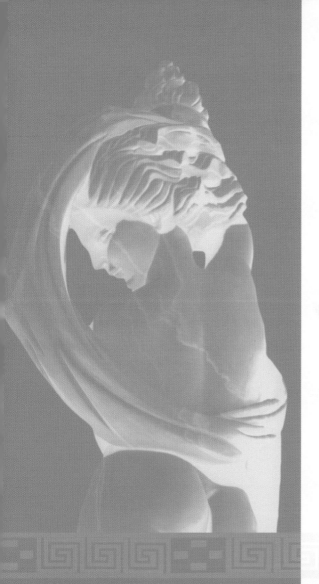

Pop Psychology

Particularly since the mid-twentieth century, psychologists and alternative healers have turned to the gods and goddesses of ancient Greece as sources of inspiration and insight into the human condition. Books such as *Goddesses in Every Woman* by Jean Shinoda Bolen and *The Goddess Within* by Jennifer and Roger Woolger view deities such as Artemis, Persephone and Aphrodite as powerful archetypes providing a path to personal growth.

Greek Drama in the Twentieth Century

In the twentieth century, themes of Greek mythology have been reinterpreted by several major dramatists. In his 1944 play *Antigone*, Jean Anouilh (1910–87) attacked the Nazis and the Vichy government while in his Orphic trilogy, Jean Cocteau (1889–1963) used film to transpose the figure of Orpheus to modern Paris and explore the role of the artist. Jean Giraudoux (1882–1944) in *Electre* and the American Eugene O'Neill (1888–1953) in *Mourning Becomes Electra* both reworked Sophocles's play, O'Neill setting it in New England in the period of the Civil War.

Modern Literature

In 1922, two key works of modernist literature appeared: *Ulysses* by James Joyce (1882–1941) and 'The Waste Land' by T.S. Eliot (1888–1965). In Joyce's novel, the events of Homer's *Odyssey* take place in a single day in Dublin, Ireland. Eliot's poem, probably the most famous of the twentieth century, also draws on Greek myth, perhaps most notably in the figure of Teiresias. Many of the poems of W.B. Yeats (1865–1939) are also inspired by Greek mythology, for example 'Leda and the Swan'. In France, André Gide (1869–1951), used Greek myth to examine the importance of the past in his philosophical novel *Theseus*.

The Gaia Hypothesis

The Gaia hypothesis, developed by scientists James Lovelock and Lynn Margulis in the 1970s, argues that the earth is a single organism. Every living thing, including human beings, is said to be part of Gaia, the Greek earth and mother goddess. The theory attracted interest and controversy in theological, scientific and environmental circles.

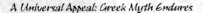

Neopagans

The gods and goddesses of ancient Greece have been given a new lease of life by members of several contemporary neo-pagan movements. Hestia and Hera are two of the most popular deities worshipped.

Language

Our everyday language makes constant reference to the gods and heroes of old. We may dream of embarking on an odyssey, notice a hectoring tone of voice, suffer from an Achilles heel, enjoy the Midas touch or even wield titanic strength. At every turn, the Greek deities confront us, embedded deep within our language and our culture.

Some Films Inspired by Greek Myths

Pygmalion (1938)	Mighty Aphrodite (1995)
Helen of Troy (1956)	The Odyssey (1997)
Jason and the Argonauts (1963)	O Brother, Where Art Thou? (2000)
My Fair Lady (1964)	Jason and the Argonauts (2000)
Ulysses (1967)	Helen of Troy (2003)
The Trojan Women 1971	Troy (2004)
Clash of the Titans 1981	Orpheus (2005)

Comics

In 1940, Captain Marvel (then called Captain Thunder) cried 'SHAZAM!' All

but the first of the letters in the magic word stands for a Greek god or hero:

Solomon, **H**eracles, **A**tlas, **Z**eus, **A**chilles, **M**ercury.

'Gods die with men who have conceived them. But the god-stuff roars

eternally, like the sea, with too vast a sound to be heard.'

D.H. Lawrence (1885–1930), *The Plumed Serpent*

A Cast of Thousands: Gods, Men and Monsters

A Cast of Thousands

More than 3,000 characters move in and out of the stories of Greek mythology. Their parentages can be tangled and disputed, their characteristics contradictory but they remain always vivid. The primal gods were the elemental deities from whom all the other deities were born, the Olympians were the gods of civilization who lived on nectar and ambrosia, and the Titans were rough, lesser beings, something like demi-gods. Hundreds of nymphs, spirits and monsters also appear, as well as mortals such as Heracles and Achilles.

The Primal Deities

Chaos (Void) neuter

Phanes (Generation) male

Phusis (Nature) or Thesis (Creation) female

Erebus (Mists of Darkness) male

Aether (Mists of Light) male

Thalassa (Sea-surface) female

Hemera (Day) female

Nyx (Night) female

Ananke (Inevitability) female

Chronus (Time) male

Gaia (Earth) female

The Ourea (Mountains) male/neuter

The Nesoi (Islands) female

Ouranos (Heaven) male

Tethys (Fresh Water) female

Oceanus (Ocean) or Hydros (water) male

Pontos (Water, the Seas) male

Tartarus (the depths of the underworld) male

Chaos, Eros and Nyx

Chaos At the very beginning of time, nothing existed, there was simply a vast emptiness known as Chaos. Some say that Chaos was the child of Mist and that Mist was the first being.

Eros In some accounts it was Eros, the god of love and sexual desire, who lit the spark that brought Chronus and Gaia together. He was often depicted carrying a bow and arrow.

Nyx An immensely powerful goddess, Nyx gave birth to many deities, usually without the help of a mate. Among her offspring were Doom, Fate, Death and Sleep. She lived in Tartarus.

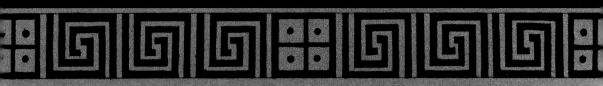

Thanatus and Erebus

Thanatus The personification of death, Thanatus was often shown armed with a sword and holding a butterfly. Sisyphus once managed to chain him up thereby preventing anyone from dying. He was eventually released by Ares, god of war.

Erebus The god of darkness who came to be identified with a region of the underworld.

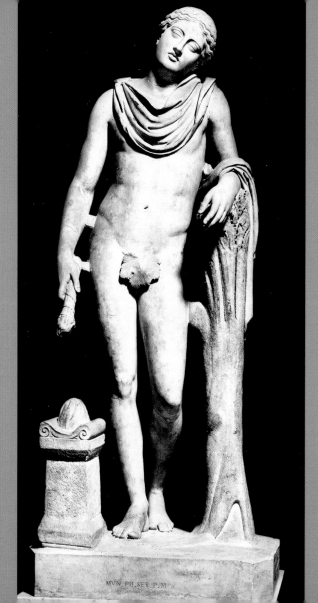

MVN.PIL.SEX.P.M.

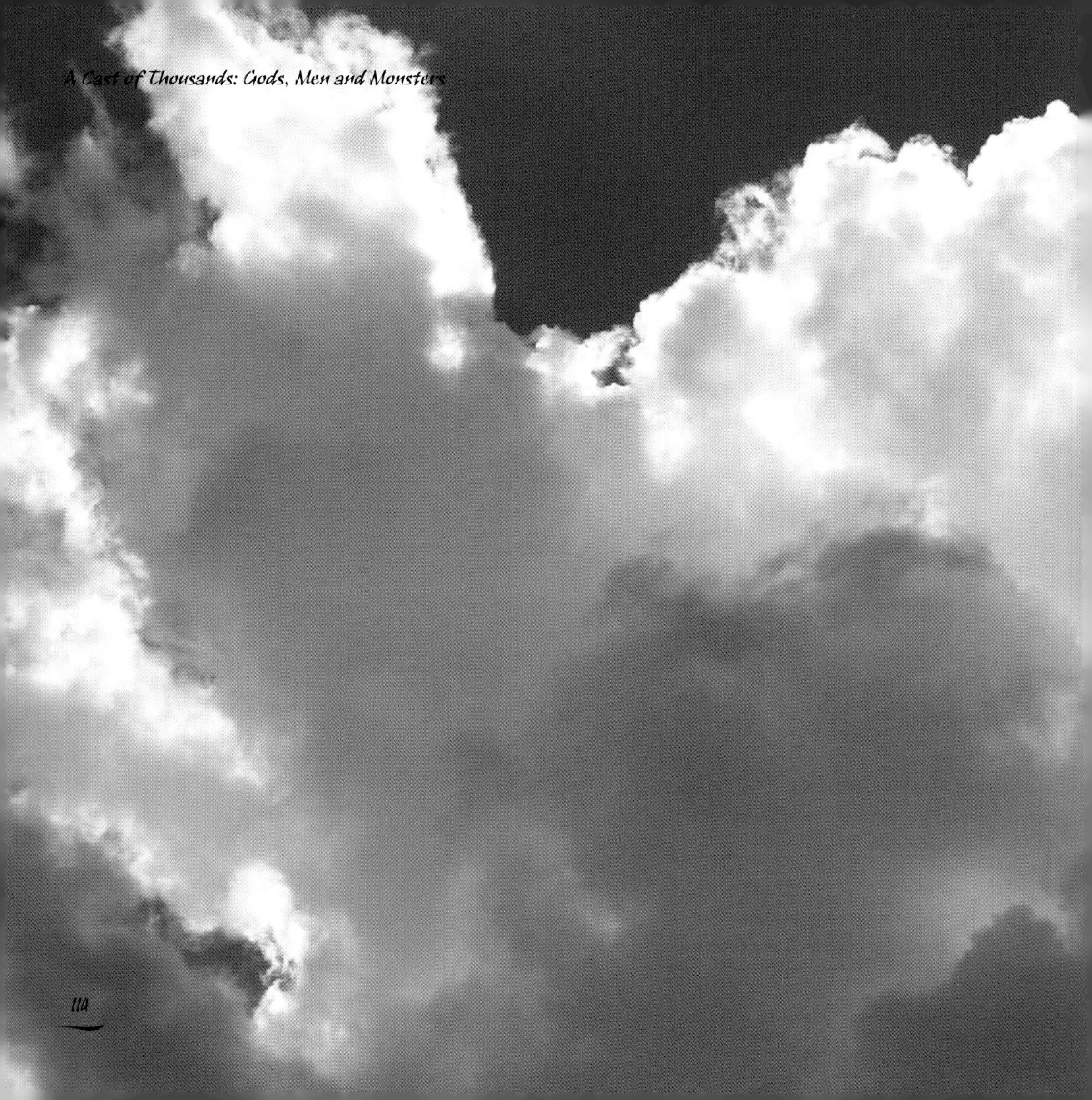

Gaia and Ouranos

Gaia The great earth goddess, Gaia was usually shown half-risen from her element. She was worshipped throughout Greece.

Ouranos The sky or heavens, Ouranos was Gaia's consort as well as her son and the first ruler of the universe. His offspring included the Titans and Cyclopes.

The Titans

Chronus and Rhea

The youngest and most terrifying Titan, Chronus was eventually overthrown by his son, Zeus. He was usually depicted with a sickle, the tool he used to castrate his father as well as to harvest crops. Rhea was the sister and consort of Chronus and the mother of Demeter, Hades, Hera, Hestia, Poseidon and Zeus. She was identified with the Anatolian mother goddess Cybele and was sometimes called Rhea Cybele or Magna Mater (great mother).

Iapetus and Clymene

A god of time and of violent death, Iapetus
allotted mortals their life-span. He and his
wife Clymene were the parents of Atlas,
Epimetheus and Prometheus.

Oceanus and Tethys

The oldest Titan, Oceanus was the great river which surrounds the earth. He and his wife, Tethys, produced all the earth's fresh water: rivers, streams, springs and rain. He was the only Titan who refused to rebel against Ouranos, his father. Tethys raised Rhea as her godchild and was also the nurse of Hera, the wife of Zeus. When Zeus placed Callisto and Arcas in the sky as the constellations Ursa Major and Ursa Minor, Hera was annoyed and so Tethys caused them to circle the sky for ever, without rest.

A Cast of Thousands: Gods, Men and Monsters

Hyperion and Theia

Hyperion was the god of light, 'he who goes before the sun'. He and Theia were the parents of Eos, the Dawn, Helius the Sun, and Selene the Moon. Theia was sometimes known as Euryphaessa (wide-shining) and was said to give precious metals and jewels their brightness. According to tradition, it was in honour of Theia that mortals turned gold into money. After the great war with Ouranos, her father, Theia took up residence in her son Helius's palace.

Mnemosyne

The Titan who presided over memory and invented words and language,

Mnemosyne preserved oral traditions before writing was invented. One story tells

how she lay with Zeus for nine nights and in due course gave birth to nine

daughters, the Muses. She had beautiful hair and a golden robe.

ΚΑΛΛΙΟΠΗ   ΚΛΕΙΩ ΕΡΑΤΩ   ΜΕΛΠΟΜΕΝΗ ΤΕΡΨΙΧΟΡΗ   ΠΟΛΥΜΝΙΑ ΕΥΤΕΡΠΕΙ   ΘΑΛΕΙΑ ΟΥΡΑΝΙΑ

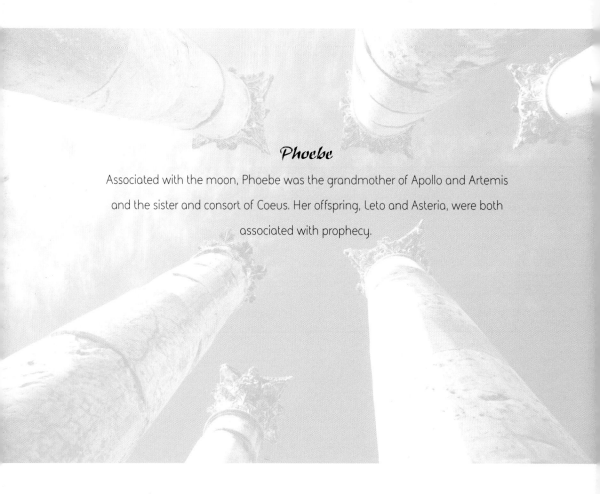

Phoebe

Associated with the moon, Phoebe was the grandmother of Apollo and Artemis and the sister and consort of Coeus. Her offspring, Leto and Asteria, were both associated with prophecy.

THEMIS.

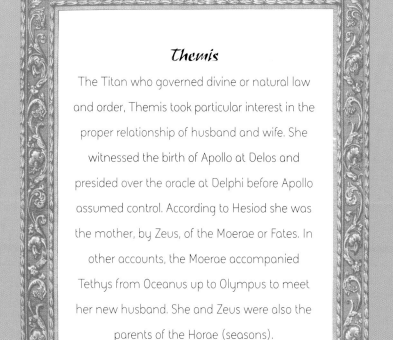

Themis

The Titan who governed divine or natural law
and order, Themis took particular interest in the
proper relationship of husband and wife. She
witnessed the birth of Apollo at Delos and
presided over the oracle at Delphi before Apollo
assumed control. According to Hesiod she was
the mother, by Zeus, of the Moerae or Fates. In
other accounts, the Moerae accompanied
Tethys from Oceanus up to Olympus to meet
her new husband. She and Zeus were also the
parents of the Horae (seasons).

Second-Generation Titans

Atlas

The son of Iapetus and Clymene, Atlas shouldered the pillars that keep heaven and earth apart, possibly in punishment for having led the Titans in their war against the Olympians. According to Ovid, he was turned into the Atlas Mountains when Perseus held the head of the Medusa before him. For a time, Heracles held up the sky in Atlas's place, releasing Atlas to help the hero in his quest for the golden apples of the Hesperides. On Atlas's return, Heracles tricked Atlas into reassuming his role.

Leto

The daughter of Coeus
and Phoebe and mother,
by Zeus, of the twins
Apollo and Artemis,
Leto protected mothers
and children.

Prometheus and Epimetheus

The sons of Iapetus and Clymene, Epimetheus's name means 'afterthought' whereas Prometheus's name means 'forethought'. According to Ovid, Prometheus moulded mortals from clay. In other accounts, he and his brother Epimetheus merely distributed characteristics and attributes among the different creatures. Prometheus stole fire and wisdom in the arts from the gods and was horribly punished for his audacity. Chained to a rock, he was condemned to have his liver pecked out by an eagle for all eternity. Heracles eventually rescued him.

Selene

Selene, the moon, was the daughter of the Titans Hyperian and Theia and the sister of Helius. She was a consort of Zeus and fell deeply in love with the youth Endymion whom Zeus then granted immortality, though in a state of everlasting sleep. She is usually represented riding a horse or driving a team of oxen, carrying a torch and wearing a crown shaped like a crescent moon on her head.

Metis

The daughter of Oceanus and Tethys, Metis was the first wife of Zeus, though she constantly tried to avoid his advances. She embodied wisdom and good counsel. When Zeus discovered she was pregnant, he swallowed her, fearing Gaia's prophecy that she would give birth to the lord of heaven. Athena later sprang from Zeus's head, fully armed.

Dione

According to some accounts,

the Titan Dione was the

mother, by Zeus, of Aphrodite.

She presided over the oracle of

Dodona in Thesprotia in

northern Greece.

The Olympians

The Olympians and their Roman Counterparts

Greek	Roman
Zeus	Jupiter
Hera	Juno
Poseidon	Neptune
Aphrodite	Venus
Demeter	Ceres
Artemis	Diana
Apollo	Apollo
Athena	Minerva
Ares	Mars
Hephaestus	Vulcan
Hermes	Mercury
Dionysus	Dionysus

Sometimes included as Olympians:

Hestia	Vesta
Hades	Pluto

Zeus

The youngest son of Chronus and Rhea, Zeus was the supreme ruler of the Olympian gods. He was the god of law, justice, the sky and weather and he had power over thunder, lightning and rain. He was famous for his numerous consorts, both mortal and divine, and his many children. His most important cult centre was at Olympia but he had numerous sanctuaries throughout Greece, often located on hill-tops or mountain peaks, and he was also worshipped privately at small household shrines. Zeus was usually portrayed as a bearded man carrying a bolt of lightning, a sceptre and an eagle.

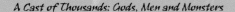

Some Consorts of Zeus

Divine

Demeter Eurynome Hera Leto Maia

Mnemosyne Selene Themis Thetis

Human

Antiope Alkmene Callisto Danae Europa

Metis Io Leda Niobe Semele

Hera

Hera was the daughter of Chronus and Rhea and the long-suffering sister and wife of Zeus. The queen of heaven, Hera ruled over the sky, women and marriage. She was the mother, by Zeus, of Hephaestus, Hebe and Ares. Each year she renewed her virginity by bathing in the Canathus spring in Argos. Fiercely jealous of Zeus, she punished his many consorts. Sometimes Zeus restrained her by chaining her to Mount Olympus, sometimes he hid his children and consorts or transformed them into animals. Women-only games were celebrated in Hera's honour at the Heraion near Mycenae, Olympia. She was portrayed as a solemn, beautiful woman.

Poseidon

The sea god Poseidon was the son of Chronus and Rhea. In Mycenaean times, he was considered more important than Zeus. He was married to the nymph Amphitrite but, like Zeus, he had many consorts and many children including Theseus, Pegasus, Pelias and Polyphemus. Poseidon lived on the floor of the ocean in a marvellous palace made of precious stones and drove a chariot pulled by horses. When he was in a good mood he calmed the sea and created new islands; when he was in a bad mood, he caused earthquakes, shipwrecks and drownings.

Hades

The ruler of the underworld and god of the dead, Hades was the son of Chronus
and Rhea. His name became synonymous with the underworld itself. Although
feared for his coldness and severity, he was not an evil god. He drove a chariot
drawn by four black horses and owned a helmet of invisibility.

Aphrodite

Aphrodite was the goddess of beauty, love, desire, pleasure and fertility. According to Homer, she was the daughter of Zeus and Dione, whereas Hesiod says she was born from the sea foam. Such was Aphrodite's beauty that Zeus quickly married her to the smith god, Hephaestus, hoping this would prevent the other gods from fighting over her. However, Hephaestus crafted a magic girdle which made the goddess even more irresistible. When Aphrodite had an affair with Ares, the sun god Helius told her husband whereupon Hephaestus trapped the two in bed together, making them a laughing stock before the other gods. Aphrodite once brought to life the statue of a woman that King Pygmalion had fallen in love with.

Aphrodite:

Incarnations and

Identifications

Astarte (Syria)

Inanna (Sumer)

Ishtar (Babylonia)

Hathor (Egypt)

Mylitta (Assyria)

Alilat (Arabia)

Venus (Roman)

Demeter

The great corn and mother goddess, Demeter was the daughter of Chronus

and Rhea and the mother, by Zeus, of Persephone. When searching for

Persephone she came to Eleusis where she was treated hospitably by King Celeus.

In gratitude, Demeter determined to make the king's son, Demophon, immortal

by holding him over a fire. One night, Demophon's mother glimpsed what was

happening and screamed whereupon Demeter dropped the child in the fire where

he burned to death. To make amends, Demeter promised to make Eleusis her

most important shrine and introduced the people to the Mysteries, that taught

initiates how to achieve happiness by overcoming fear of death.

Artemis

The daughter of Zeus and Leto, Artemis

was the virgin goddess of hunting and

wild animals. She was usually shown

armed with a bow and arrows.

Apollo

The god of prophecy, poetry, music, inspiration and healing, Apollo was the son of Zeus and Leto. He was born on the floating island of Delos, the site of one of his two most important shrines, the other being at Delphi. Usually known as 'the bright one', Apollo was depicted as a handsome, beardless youth with long hair and various attributes including a wreath, a laurel branch, a lyre and a bow. He captured Tityus the giant who attacked Leto, and he punished Niobe, queen of Thebes, for boasting that she was superior to Leto, by killing her six sons while his sister Artemis killed her six daughters.

Athena

The great goddess of wisdom, intelligence and crafts, Athena was born, fully armed, from the head of Zeus after he had swallowed the pregnant Metis, goddess of wisdom. In a contest with Poseidon for control of Athens, Athena created the olive tree and afterwards introduced the art of its cultivation. She presided over the first case of murder when Orestes was tried for killing his mother Clytemnestra. During the Trojan War, Athena helped the Greeks, annoyed that in his famous Judgement, Paris had named Aphrodite the most beautiful goddess. She was usually shown wearing a helmet and armed with a shield and spear.

Ares

The son of Zeus and Hera, Ares was the god of war and bloodlust. He was the adulterous lover of Aphrodite and killed Adonis, his rival for her affections, after transforming himself into a boar. He fathered the female warriors called the Amazons by the nymph Harmonia.

Dionysus

The son of Zeus and Semele, a mortal woman, Dionysus was the god of wine and frenzy. Jealous Hera drove him mad and sent him out to wander the world until at last Zeus healed him. Scorned by the women of Thebes, Dionysus incited them to such a frenzy that, at its height, the mother of King Pentheus tore her son limb from limb. Later, when the women of Argos refused to worship him, Dionysus drove them insane whereupon they ate their own children. Dionysus finally fell in love with Ariadne whom Theseus had abandoned. He was sometimes shown as a beautiful youth accompanied by Satyrs and Maenads.

Hermes

Renowned above all as the messenger of Zeus, Hermes was also the god of roads, travel, writing, wit, language, and much more besides. The son of Zeus and Maia, the eldest of the Pleiades, he was born in Arcadia. A type of trickster god, he invented the lyre and on the very day of his birth he stole Apollo's cows. He carried messages from the gods to humans and accompanied the dead on their way to the afterlife. He was usually shown as a handsome young man wearing winged sandals and sometimes a winged cap.

Pan

Though not an original or true Olympian, Pan's parentage is uncertain and he is often grouped with the gods of Olympus. The god of shepherds, woods, fields, and mountains, Pan was born with a beard and pointed ears. His nurse took fright at the sight of him, hence the word panic. Irrepressibly lecherous, he often dallied with nymphs and Maenads. Both Sirynx and Pitys became plants to escape his advances; Sirynx turned into a clump of reeds from which Pan crafted his famous pipes. A very ancient god, Pan came to be seen as the son of either Hermes or Zeus; his mother was a nymph. He had the horns, feet and tail of a goat all of which probably contributed to images of the Christian Satan.

Hephaestus

The son of Zeus and Hera, or possibly of Hera alone, Hephaestus was the god of fire,

metalwork and the fine arts. He was born with a shrivelled foot which made Hera so

ashamed that she threw him out of Olympus whereupon Thetis and Eurynome, a

daughter of Oceanus, looked after him. Later, Hephaestus gained his revenge by

crafting a magnificent throne which he sent to Hera. When the goddess sat in it she was immediately trapped; Hephaestus only released her after Dionysus had made him drunk. Hephaestus also fashioned Pandora, the first woman. He was married to Aphrodite, though she, thinking him ugly, preferred Ares.

Hestia

The virgin goddess of hearth and home,
Hestia was the oldest child of Chronus and
Rhea. She begged Zeus to be allowed to
remain a virgin and he granted her wish,
saying that she should preside over sacrifices
and be at the centre of every home.

178

ΚΑΛΛΙΟΠΗ   ΚΛΕΙΩ ΕΡΑΤΩ   ΜΕΛΠΟΜΕΝΗ 798

Monsters, Muses and Other Beings

The Muses

The offspring of the Titaness Mnemosyne, the Muses were goddesses of music, song, dance and inspiration. They usually sang for the gods but sometimes for heroes.

Calliope	Epic poetry
Clio	History
Ourania	Astronomy
Thaleia	Comedy
Melpomene	Tragedy
Polyhymnia	Religious hymns
Erato	Erotic poetry
Euterpe	Lyric poetry
Terpsichore	Choral song and dance

179

The Pleiades (Seven Sisters)

The daughters of Atlas and Pleione, the gods placed

the Pleiades in the sky so that they could escape

Orion's advances. They were:

Alcyone

Celaeno

Electra

Maia

Merope

Sterope

Taygete

The Moerae (Fates)

Clotho spun the thread of life.

Lachesis measured the thread of life.

Atropos (or Aisa) cut the thread of life.

The Erinyes (Furies)

The Erinyes were three ugly, winged goddesses called Alecto, Megaera and Tisiphone, born either from the blood of Ouranos, or from Nyx. It was their job to avenge crimes, particularly murder and impiety, by inflicting madness, famine or disease on the offender.

Monsters and Giants

Echidna A she-dragon with the upper body of a nymph.

Gorgons Three terrifying sisters with snakes twining around their heads, wings, and claws. Medusa was the only mortal Gorgon.

The Minotaur A bull-headed monster, the child of Queen Pasiphae of Crete, conceived when she fell in love with a bull.

Graeae Three hags, born old, who had only one eye and one tooth to share between them.

Harpies Winged monsters with the bodies of birds and heads of women.

Hydra A nine-headed snake that grew another two heads for every one that was cut off.

Chimaera A monster with three heads, the front of a lion, the back of a goat and the tail of a serpent.

The Sirens Half-birds, half-women, they lived by the sea and lured sailors onto the rocks with their music so that they capsized and drowned.

Cyclopes One-eyed giants led by Polyphemus.

Heroes and Warriors

Achilles

The son of the mortal Peleus, king of the Myrmidons, and Thetis, a sea nymph,
Achilles was the greatest Greek in the Trojan War and the central character in
Homer's *Iliad*. Thetis tried to make Achilles immortal. In one version she
attempted to burn away his mortality but was interrupted by Peleus; in the other,
she dipped him in the river Styx but failed to douse the heel she held him by.
Knowing he would die in the Trojan War, she hid Achilles away, disguised as a girl.

TO ARTHUR. DUKE OF WELLINGTON.
AND HIS BRAVE COMPANIONS IN ARMS
THE STATUE OF ACHILLES
CAST FROM CANNON TAKEN IN THE VICTORIES
OF SALAMANCA. VITTORIA. TOULOUSE. AND WATERLOO.
IS INSCRIBED
BY THEIR COUNTRYWOMEN.

Achilles and Hector

Calchas the seer had prophesied that Troy would not fall without Achilles' help and
so Odysseus tracked the young man down. At Troy, Agamemnon took Achilles's
war-slave away from him whereupon Achilles was so angry that he refused to
fight. Eventually, however, he allowed his friend Patroclus to take his place in battle
and lent him his armour. Hector, son of King Priam of Troy, killed Patroclus
whereupon, grief-stricken, Achilles returned to battle. Achilles finally killed Hector,
then desecrated his body by dragging it around the walls of Troy. Priam's son
Paris killed Achilles by shooting him in the ankle with an arrow.

Jason

Jason was the son of Aeson, the rightful King of Iolcos. Pelias had seized the throne from Aeson but lived in fear of a prophecy that someone would harm him. When Pelias realized Jason was that person, he sent the youth off to bring back the Golden Fleece from Colchis. Jason returned successful, helped greatly by Medea, the King of Colchis's daughter. Back in Iolcos, Medea used her cunning to have Pelias killed. Afterwards, she and Jason fled to Corinth where Jason married the king's daughter. Medea took a terrible revenge, even killing her own children.

Heracles

The son of Zeus and the mortal Alkmene, Heracles was incredibly strong and brave. While still a baby, he strangled two serpents bare-handed. After countless exploits, Heracles died from a poisoned tunic. On his funeral pyre, he was struck by lighting and was transformed into a god on Olympus. He married Hebe, goddess of youth.

Bellerophon

The son of King Glaucus of Corinth,

Bellerophon was a prodigious horseman.

He determined to kill the monster

Chimaera and was assisted by Athena

who gave him a marvellous horse,

Pegasus. Unfortunately, Bellerophon

overstepped himself whereupon he was

punished by Zeus.

Theseus

Theseus was the son of princess Aethra of Troizan and either King Aegeus of Athens or the sea god Poseidon. Medea, the wife of Aegeus, tried to have Theseus killed but he survived and performed many brave deeds. He is said to have brought democracy to Attica, where Athens is situated.

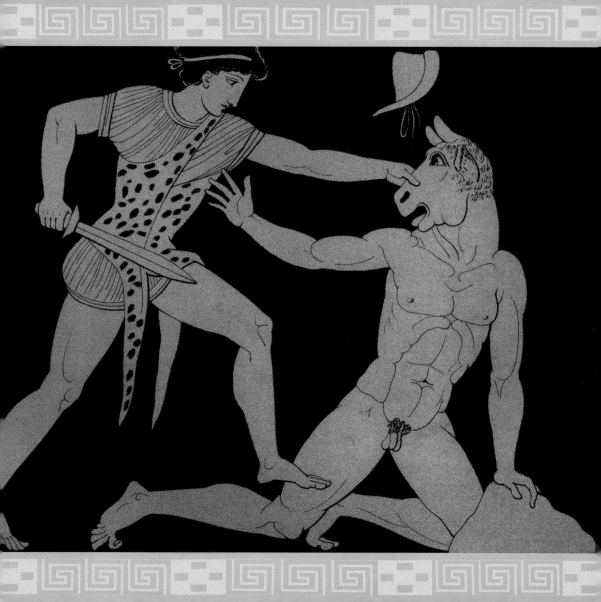

Odysseus

The hero of Homer's *Odyssey*, Odysseus was clever as well as brave. He was one of Helen's original suitors and, when Paris abducted Helen, he was called on to fight in the Trojan War. At first, Odysseus pretended to be mad since an oracle had told him it would be many years before he returned home. However, his pretence was discovered whereupon he set out for war, fought heroically and, according to some accounts, thought up the idea of the Trojan Horse. As predicted, it took Odysseus ten years to return home to his wife Penelope.

Perseus

Perseus was the son of Zeus and Danae, the daughter of King Acrisius of Argos. An oracle had told Acrisius that he would be killed by his grandson and so he locked Danae in a metal chamber. However, Zeus entered the chamber as a shower of golden rain and, in due course, Danae bore a son, Perseus. Acrisius threw mother and child into the sea in a wooden crate but they eventually drifted to land and escaped. Perseus became famous for rescuing Andromeda and slaughtering Medusa, a gorgon. According to one account, he killed his grandfather by accident when throwing a quoit. He later founded the city of Mycenae.

Amazons

The Amazons were female warriors who were said to kill men. They lived near the river Thermodon in Anatolia, which is now northern Turkey, and worshipped Artemis and Ares. According to legend, they removed their right breasts so that they could shoot their arrows more easily.

Creation, Quest, Transformation and Family

Creation Myths

The Creation of the Primal Gods and the Titans

First of all came Chaos; next came Gaia, the Earth, dim Tartarus, fair Eros, dark Erebus, and Night. Then Night coupled with Erebus and produced Aether, the bright air, and Day. Afterwards, Earth gave birth to Ouranos, the starry heaven, so that he could provide a safe home for the blessed gods. Then Earth created the hills and Pontos, the raging deep. Next, Earth lay with Ouranos and gave birth to Oceanus, Coeus and Crius, Hyperion and Iapetus, Theia and Rhea, Themis and Mnemosyne, Phoebe and Tethys. Finally, Earth gave birth to Chronus, the most terrible of her children. And Chronus hated Ouranos.

The Giants

After giving birth to the gods and Titans, Gaia, the great earth mother, bore three one-eyed giants called Cyclopes. Next, she gave birth to three monsters each with fifty heads and a hundred arms. These giants were the most terrible children of Ouranos and Gaia. From the very beginning, their father hated them.

The Son with the Sickle

Angry that Ouranos hated her children, Gaia
hatched a terrifying plot. Of all her offspring,
only Chronus was brave enough to see it
through. Gaia gave him a great sickle made
of flint, then told him to hide himself and lie
in wait. That night, when Ouranos came to
lie with Gaia, Chronus jumped out of hiding,
lopped off his father's genitals and threw
them into the sea.

The Birth of Aphrodite

The blood of Ouranos spattered down to earth and from its drops came the Erinyes, Giants and Nymphs. Meanwhile, the god's severed genitals fell into the sea where they were swept away in a mound of white foam. Slowly, a beautiful maiden, the goddess Aphrodite, grew within the foam and drifted gently over the waves until at last she came to rest at Cyprus.

The Lesser Gods and the Olympians

The Titans gave birth to many lesser gods and goddesses. Coeus and Phoebe became the parents of Leto, Hecate and Asteria while Rhea and Chronus produced Hestia, Demeter, Hera, Hades and wise Zeus. Chronus had learnt from Gaia and Ouranos that he would be overthrown by his own son and so he swallowed his children the moment they were born. He also imprisoned his Titan brothers and sisters.

Creation, Quest, Transformation and Family

The Birth of Zeus

The next time Rhea came close to giving birth, she begged her parents for help. Gaia and Ouranos sent her to a safe haven on the island of Crete and it was there that Zeus was born. The moment the baby arrived in the world, Gaia hid him in a remote cave, then hurried to Chronus carrying a stone wrapped in swaddling clothes. Chronus seized the stone and, thinking it was Rhea's child, swallowed it. Years passed by and eventually Chronus vomited up the children he had swallowed.

The Clash of the Titans

Zeus eventually released the Titans from
where Chronus had imprisoned them and they, in
their gratitude, gave him thunder and lightning. Soon,
however, a war broke out between the Titans and Olympians,
a fierce, seemingly endless battle called the Titanomachy. Then
Zeus sought the help of the three hundred-armed giants called
the Hecatoncheires, and the whole world shook and Olympus
itself trembled. Zeus rushed forwards hurling his lightning
bolt whereupon the seas boiled, flames rose up and
the Hecatoncheires buried the Titans beneath
rocks and bound them in chains.

The Rule of Zeus

After the fall of the Titans, Gaia gave birth to Typhoeus, an enormously strong god with a hundred snake heads, each with a flickering tongue, eyes that flashed fire and a hundred dreadful voices. This terrifying god would have become lord of all mankind if Zeus had not leapt from Olympus, struck him down and cast him into Tartarus. Now that their struggles were over at last, the gods of Olympus begged Zeus to be their leader and so he ruled over them as king of heaven and earth.

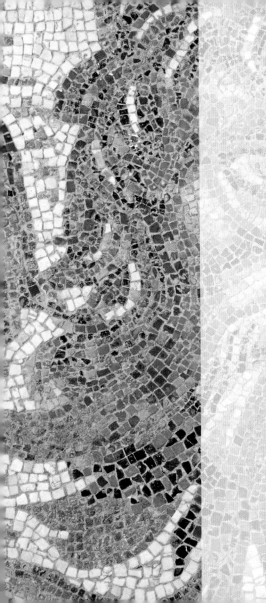

Homer's Creation

According to Homer, Oceanus is 'the primal source of

all that lives ... from whom the gods are sprung'.

The Orphic Creation Myth

In the very beginning there was a being called Phanes, 'The One who makes Appear' or 'The One who Appears'. Phanes emerged from a cosmic egg created by Time. The top half of the egg became the heavens and the bottom half the earth. Phanes embodied everything that was male and everything that was female and everything that was to come. Indeed, he was the first king of the entire universe. He was succeeded by Nyx, his only child, and then by Ouranos. In due course, Chronus seized power from Ouranos and then Chronus was succeeded by Zeus. Finally, Zeus devoured Phanes to ensure that he himself assumed complete power. Some say that Phanes had four heads, others that he was a beautiful, golden-winged deity, half male, half female. Whether or not this was so we do not know for he was invisible, even to the gods.

'Firstly, black-winged Night laid a germless egg in the bosom of
the infinite deeps of Erebus, and from this, after the revolution of
long ages, sprang the graceful Eros with his glittering golden
wings, swift as the whirlwinds of the tempest.'

Aristophanes, *The Birds*, 414 BC

*Orphism was a mystery religion allegedly founded by the poet
Orpheus and active from about the sixth century BC.*

The Pelasgian Creation Myth

Long ago, at the very beginning of time, the great serpent Ophion ruled the world alongside Eurynome, daughter of Oceanus. Time passed, and at last the divine couple were deposed by Chronus and Rhea. Down they fell, way down, deep into the sea.

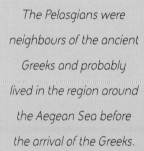

The Pelasgians were neighbours of the ancient Greeks and probably lived in the region around the Aegean Sea before the arrival of the Greeks.

The Creation of Man — The Five Ages

Many civilizations have conceived of the past as being divided into a series of

different ages. According to Hesiod, there were five such divisions. The first, the

Golden Age, was ruled by Chronus whereas the others were all ruled by Zeus.

The Golden Age

The first age, the Golden Age, was an age when people lived like gods in an everlasting present. It was an age of happiness, trust, innocence and perpetual spring. The earth provided food in abundance and people ate no meat. Eventually the Golden Age, a lost paradise, came to an end.

The Silver Age

This was an age of suffering and hardship when men and women refused to offer sacrifices to the gods and sinned without cease. People now had to work for a living with the ox and plough and, after Zeus introduced the seasons, they were uncomfortably hot in summer and cold in winter. When they died, they lived under the earth as spirits.

The Bronze Age

In the Bronze Age, people began to fight and eat meat. They wore bronze
armour, lived in bronze houses and used tools made from bronze. This was a
period of war, violence and savagery. Justice fled from the world forever and
people became hard-hearted. When they died, they went to Hades.

240

The Heroic Age

This was a nobler and better age than the Bronze Age. Zeus created a god-like

race of heroes from whose ranks came the bravest soldiers of the Trojan War.

Mortals still perished but some of the greatest heroes survived to live on the

Islands of the Blessed in a perpetual Golden Age.

The Iron Age

We now live in the Iron Age, the antithesis of the Golden Age. Where there was pleasure, now there is pain, where there was love, now there is hate, where there was peace now there is war. The wicked rule the good, families fight amongst themselves and nobody can be trusted.

The Orphic Creation of Man

The Birth of Zagreus

During the terrifying war between the Titans and the gods of Olympos, Demeter hid her daughter Persephone in a cave for safekeeping. Zeus spied her there and, taking the form of a snake, he forced himself on her. The resulting child, a boy, was called Zagreus. While still an infant, Zagreus climbed onto Zeus's throne and waved the great king's lightning bolts around. Zeus's wife, Hera, was fiercely jealous and persuaded the Titans to cook and eat the boy. While Zagreus examined himself in a mirror, the Titans crept up and cut him into pieces. However, Zeus managed to save his son's heart.

ΗΦΑΙΣΙΟΣ   ΔΙΟΝ

The Birth of Dionysus

Zeus made a potion from the heart of
Zagreus and gave it to Semele, a mortal
woman, to drink. In due course Semele
gave birth to Dionysus, the second-born.
Meanwhile, Zeus was so furious with the
Titans that he struck them with bolts of
thunder and lightning. Mortals were
formed from their ashes.

Plato's Creation of Man

Long ago only the gods existed. When the time came for mortal creatures to be made, the gods fashioned them out of earth and fire. Their work done, the gods ordered Prometheus and his brother Epimetheus to equip the creatures with attributes. Epimetheus volunteered to perform the task, asking Prometheus to inspect his work. So Epimetheus distributed various qualities among the creatures, leaving mankind until last. When the time came for him to give men their qualities, he realized he had nothing at all left. At this point, Prometheus arrived to inspect his brother's work and was horrified to see that men lacked some of their basic requirements. It was almost time for the people to be sent out into the world and so Prometheus gave them fire, which he stole from the gods. He also stole craft and metalworking skills for them.

Pandora, the First Woman

Zeus was angry with Prometheus for having

stolen fire from the gods and decided to take

revenge. At his bidding, the smith god Hephaestus

fashioned a girl from earth and water. Athena

decked the lovely creature out in a silvery gown

with a veil and flowers and taught her needlework

and weaving; Aphrodite gave her grace and

longing. Finally, Hermes gave the girl deceitfulness

and speech and called her Pandora (All Gifts).

Pandora was so beautiful that she entranced

everyone who saw her but she had an evil nature

and was the source of all sorrow. All women must

claim their descent from her.

The Introduction of Evil

Hermes gave Pandora to Epimetheus as a gift. Prometheus had told his brother that he must never accept a present from Zeus, but Epimetheus ignored the advice. Pandora brought with her a jar. The moment she took off its lid, all the sorrows and plagues of the world flew out. Only Hope remained.

The Flood

Prometheus had a son called Deucalion who married Pyrrha, the daughter of Epimetheus and Pandora. Realizing that Zeus wanted to destroy the people of the Bronze Age in a terrifying flood, Prometheus told Deucalion to build a chest, fill it with provisions and climb inside, together with Pyrrha. Soon afterwards, Zeus flooded the earth with torrential rains. For nine days and nine nights, Deucalion and Pyrrha floated on the waters in their chest. Eventually, they landed on Mount Parnassus, the rain stopped and Deucalion climbed out, gave thanks to Zeus, and performed sacrifices.

Re-populating the Earth

Zeus sent Hermes down to earth to ask Deucalion if there was
anything in particular he wanted, whereupon Deucalion asked to be
given men. At Zeus's bidding, Deucalion and Pyrrha threw stones
over their shoulders. The stones that Deucalion threw became men
whereas the stones that Pyrrha threw became women.

Creation of the Spartoi

Following the advice of the Delphic oracle, Cadmus, son of the Phoenician king, determined to found a city where a particular cow lay down to rest. The cow eventually lay down whereupon Cadmus prepared to sacrifice the beast to Athena. He sent his companions to draw water from a spring but a dragon sprang out and killed most of them. In retaliation, Cadmus killed the dragon and, on the advice of Athena, sowed its teeth in the ground. Armed warriors rose from the ground where the teeth had been sown. Some of them killed each other but five survived. The city Cadmus founded was called Thebes. The men were the Spartoi.

Demeter, Persephone and the Arrival of the Seasons

One day, Persephone was wandering through the meadows picking flowers – roses, violets and narcissi. She reached out to touch a narcissus whereupon the earth sprang open and out rushed Hades. He pulled Persephone into his golden chariot and charged back to his realm of darkness. Only Hecate and Helius heard her screams.

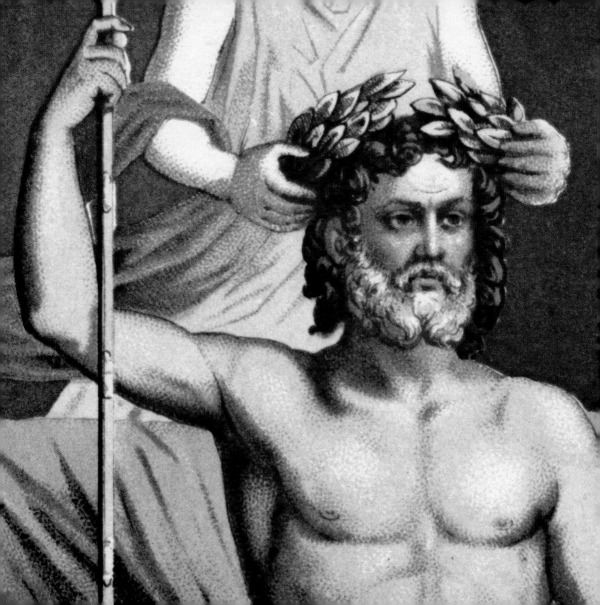

Demeter Disappears

Sensing something was wrong, Demeter sped across land and sea in search of her daughter. When Helius told her what had happened, she abandoned Olympus and moved to the city of Eleusis where she began to waste away with grief. That year, nothing grew. One by one, the gods begged Demeter to return, but she refused. Finally, Zeus sent Hermes to ask Hades to release Persephone. Anxious not to offend the gods, Hades agreed. However, he secretly slipped Persephone some pomegranate seeds to eat: he knew that anyone who ate food in the underworld must stay there forever.

Persephone's Release

At long last, Persephone set out for the upper world. When Demeter saw her, she rushed towards her like a madwoman. Zeus decreed that since Persephone had eaten only a few pomegranate seeds, she need only spend a third of each year in the underworld. Each spring, Persephone would rise from the realm of darkness and stay with her mother and the other immortals. Reunited with her daughter, Demeter finally allowed the crops to grow so that the entire earth was laden with leaves and blossoms.

Heroes and Quests

The Labours of Heracles

Hera always treated Zeus's illegitimate offspring badly and Heracles was no exception. Once, she cursed him with a fit of madness during which he slaughtered his wife and children. To atone for his crime the great hero had to complete twelve punishing tasks set by Eurystheus, king of Tiryns.

The Nemean Lion

The first task was to kill the vicious lion that lived in Nemea, a monster which

no weapon could wound. Heracles finally succeeded in strangling the beast.

The Lernaean Hydra

Heracles had to slay the nine-headed Hydra, a monster which grew new

heads each time one was cut off. He succeeded by searing each neck.

The Ceryneian Stag

The hero had to bring the gold-antlered stag back to Eurystheus alive.

It took him a whole year to capture the beast.

The Erymanthian Boar

Heracles chased the monster until it collapsed

with exhaustion. Terrified, Eurystheus hid from

it in an urn.

The Augean Stables

The task was to clean the vast and filthy

stables in a single day. Heracles performed the

task by diverting the rivers Alpheus and Peneus.

The Stymphalian Birds

The monstrous metal-winged creatures

plagued the people of Arcadia.

Athena drove them into the sky whereupon

Heracles shot them down, one by one.

Creation Quest: Transformations Eternity

The Cretan Bull

The formidable bull terrorized Crete.
Heracles brought it back alive to Eurystheus.

The Mares of Diomedes

These monstrous, man-eating creatures
belonged to King Diomedes. Heracles killed
the king, fed him to his horses, then led the
creatures to Eurystheus.

The Girdle of Hippolyte

Hippolyte would willingly have given
Heracles the girdle but Hera stirred up
trouble so that Heracles had to kill the
queen before winning his prize.

The Cattle of Geryon

Heracles drove the famous red cattle to Eurystheus after killing the
giant Geryon as well as his terrifying herdsman and hound.

The Apples of the Hesperides

With the help of Atlas, Heracles managed to return from the distant
isle with the fabulous golden apples, guarded by the dragon Ladon.

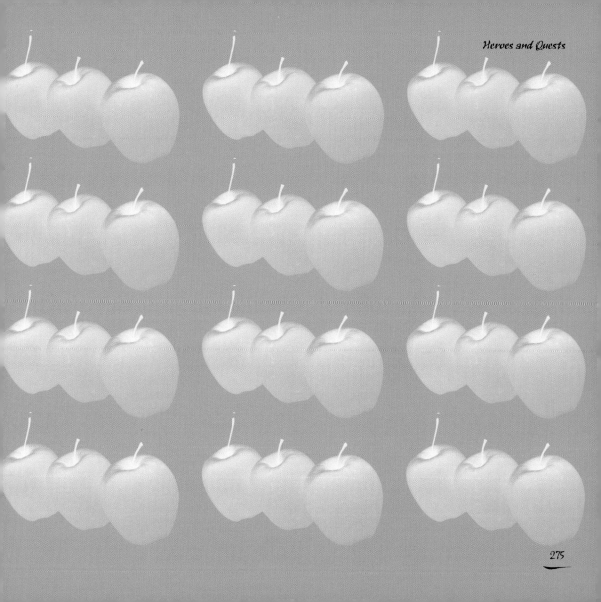

Cerberus, the final labour

Heracles's final task was to bring Eurystheus the three-headed dog Cerberus which guarded the gates of the underworld. After presenting the terrifying creature to the king, Heracles took the beast back to the underworld. Now that his labours were completed, Heracles had at last atoned for his sins.

Jason and the Argonauts

Jason's task was to bring Pelias, the wicked king of Iolcus, the precious Golden Fleece. The fleece came from the magic flying ram that had helped Phrixus and Helle and was now guarded by a dragon in the land of Colchis. If Jason completed the task, Pelias promised that he would grant him his rightful place on the throne of Iolcus.

The Argo

Jason's ship, the Argo, was built by Argus with the help of either Athena or Hera. It incorporated a branch from Zeus's sacred oak tree. Among the fifty Argonauts were many illustrious heroes including Heracles, Orpheus, the twins Castor and Polydeuces and Peleus, the father of Achilles.

Lemnos

The Argonauts' first stop was Lemnos, an island inhabited by women so fierce they had killed all their men. However, the women welcomed the Argonauts and invited them to help repopulate the island. Jason fathered twins by the queen and, before leaving, the women gave the Argonauts food, wine and clothing.

kyzicos

The Argnoauts were well treated here by the local king who was especially

grateful when Heracles rid the land of giants. After leaving, the Argonauts were

driven back to shore by fierce winds. It was dark and the people rushed at the ship, not recognizing its occupants, whereupon the Argonauts massacred them.

Mysia

This was where Hylas, the companion of Heracles, was lured away

by a nymph whereupon Heracles refused to continue the voyage.

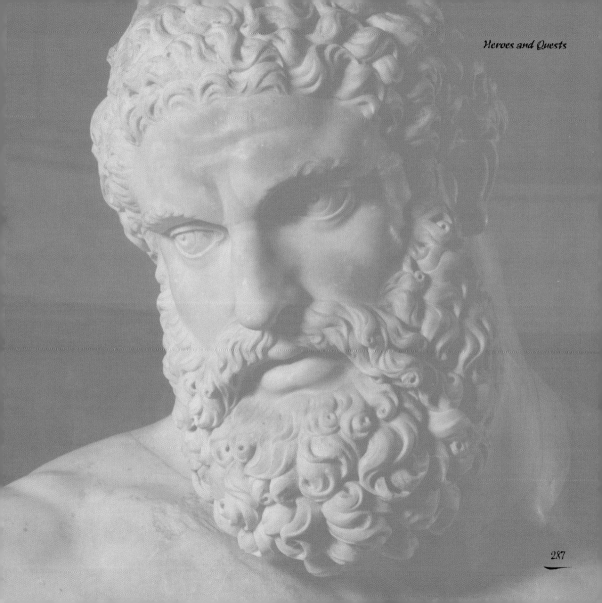

Bebryces

King Amycus of Bebryces was a skilled
boxer who challenged all visitors to fight
him to the death. Polydeuces accepted
and killed him.

Salymydessus

Here Jason met the blind old king Phineus who had been
given the gift of prophecy by Apollo but was plagued
eternally by the horrible bird-like creatures the Harpies in
punishment for having revealed the intentions of the gods to
mortals. Jason killed the Harpies and, in return, Phineus told
him how to reach Colchis.

Colchis

King Aeetes agreed to give Jason the Golden
Fleece provided he performed certain tasks.
Meanwhile, Hera and Aphrodite agreed to
make the king's daughter, Medea, fall in love
with Jason. The king told Jason to yoke two
terrifying bulls, plough a field and sow it with
the teeth of a dragon. These teeth would
become armed men and Jason must kill them.
Medea gave Jason a magic potion which would
make him invincible for a day and thereby
Jason completed the task. Enraged, King Aeetes
decided to break his promise and kill Jason.
Medea drugged the dragon that guarded the
Golden Fleece and that very night they seized
the fleece and made their escape.

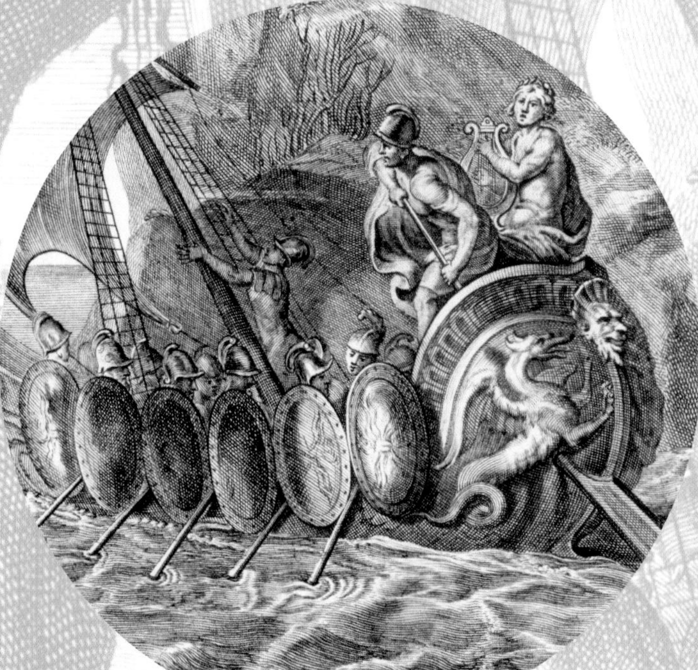

The Return

The Argonauts quickly put to sea but King Aeetes made chase. To slow him down, Medea killed her brother and flung pieces of his corpse into the water. Aeetes was honour-bound to stop and gather them. Further along their way, the Argonauts were nearly seduced by the beautiful voices of the deadly Sirens but Orpheus made even more beautiful music, blocking out their sound. Nearing home, they passed the island of Crete where a bronze giant, Talus, tried to sink their boat by throwing rocks at it. However, Medea cast a spell on Talus so that he bled to death.

Iolcus

Back at Iolcus, Medea told King Pelias's daughters that they could make their father young again by chopping him into pieces and boiling him in a cauldron. She demonstrated with a lamb but secretly added magic herbs to the cauldron. The daughters did as bidden but Medea added no magic herbs and so Pelias died a horrible death. Jason and Medea settled in Corinth, driven out of Iolcus by Pelias's son. Theirs was not a happy life, steeped as it was in trickery and dishonour. Jason died, old and sad, when a plank from the rotting Argo fell on him.

Theseus and the Minotaur

King Minos of Crete ordered the Athenians to send him seven of their maidens and seven of their youths every nine years so that they might be fed to the monstrous Minotaur. The Minotaur lived in the Labyrinth, a vast maze where victims perished through fear and starvation if they escaped being eaten.

The Tribute

The time for the next payment came around whereupon Theseus, the son of the Athenian king, volunteered to be one of the victims. Off he sailed with the other young people, promising that when the ship returned it should fly a white sail if he were still alive and a black one if he were dead.

The Family of Minos

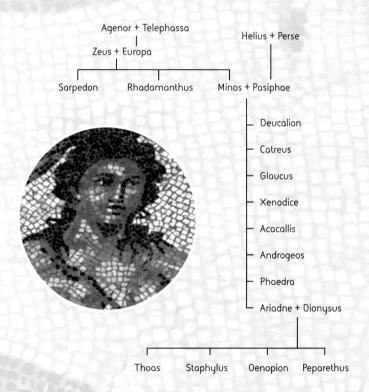

Agenor + Telephassa
|
Zeus + Europa

Helius + Perse

Sarpedon — Rhadamanthus — Minos + Pasiphae

- Deucalion
- Catreus
- Glaucus
- Xenodice
- Acacallis
- Androgeos
- Phaedra
- Ariadne + Dionysus

Thoas — Staphylus — Oenopion — Peparethus

Ariadne

When Theseus arrived in Crete, Ariadne, daughter of King Minos, fell desperately in love with him. She told him how he might escape from the Labyrinth by following the thread of a ball of twine. So Theseus killed the Minotaur, escaped from the Labyrinth and sailed back to Athens with Ariadne and the maidens and youths. On his way home, Theseus abandoned Ariadne on the island of Naxos, maybe by accident or maybe in a deliberate act of cruelty. Nearing his native shore, he forgot to switch his ship's sail whereupon his father, Aegeus, presumed Theseus dead and so threw himself into the sea. Theseus succeeded him as King of Athens.

The Trojan Horse

The Greeks had laid siege to Troy for ten years without gaining entrance to the city, when at last, according to most legends, Odysseus came up with an idea: they would build a huge wooden horse, secretly fill its hollow belly with warriors and leave it standing in front of the city walls. So, while a few brave warriors hid inside the horse, the remaining Greeks burnt their camps and pretended to sail away. When the Trojans looked out, all they saw was the vast horse standing there. Despite dire warnings from Laocoon and Cassandra, they eagerly pulled it inside their city walls, believing it to be an offering to the goddess Athena.

The Trojan Victory

That night, while the Trojan warriors lay in a drunken stupor after celebrating their imagined victory, forty or so Greek warriors climbed down from inside the wooden horse's hollow belly. Silently, they opened the gates of Troy to the Greek army which had sailed back to shore. The next morning, all but a few Trojans were dead. Priam had been killed as well as Hector's young son, Astyanax, who had been thrown from the city walls. Only a few helpless women remained.

The Wanderings of Odysseus

At the very end of the Trojan War, the Greeks angered the gods by desecrating Troy's altars. To punish them, the gods scattered their fleet as they sailed for home. The ships of Odysseus, King of Ithaca, became separated from the rest of the fleet and he and his men entered a terrifying world of monsters.

The Lotus Eaters,
Polyphemus and king Aeolus

The first great set-back Odysseus encountered
was on the island of the Lotus Eaters where his
men were entranced with sweet fruits of
forgetfulness. After managing to drag them
away, they came to the land of the Cyclopes
where the one-eyed giant Polyphemus trapped
them in his cave. Odysseus blinded the monster
and he and his men managed to escape by
clinging on to the underbellies of sheep.

After this, the king of the the floating island
Aeolia gave them a bag of winds to help them
on their homeward journey. When they had
nearly reached Ithaca, a sailor opened the bag
and the winds blew them back, almost as far as
where they had started from.

More Monsters

Odysseus and his men came next to the land of the Laestrygonians who killed and ate all but Odysseus's own crew. Further along, on the island of Aeaea, they were greeted by the enchantress Circe who changed Odysseus's men into pigs. Once again, Odysseus came to the rescue. Afterwards, he persuaded Circe to help him find the way to Hades where the seer Teiresias would reveal his fate to him. After learning that he was to die in old age, Odysseus sailed past the Sirens, having blocked his men's ears with wax and tied himself to the mast in order to withstand their beseeching voices.

Scylla, Charybdis and Calypso

Soon afterwards, the monstrous Scylla managed to

snatch some of Odysseus's crew but Odysseus pressed onwards,

sailing between Scylla and the whirlpool Charybdis, coming next to

the island of Thrinacia. There, his men slaughtered the Cattle of Helius,

for which crime Zeus destroyed Odysseus's ship and killed all that were

left of his crew. All alone now, Odysseus came to the island of the

nymph Calypso who kept him with her for seven years. Even though

Calypso offered Odysseus immortality if he stayed with her, the

hero insisted on returning home to Penelope, his wife. He

escaped on a raft which was eventually washed up

on the shores of the Phaeacians.

Ithaca

The King of the Phaeacians gave Odysseus a fleet and provisions so that he could return home in comfort. Back in Ithaca, the great hero found his lands laid to waste and countless suitors pestering for the hand of his wife. Penelope had promised to marry again when she had finished weaving her tapestry but each night she secretly undid some of her work. The suitors had now grown impatient and so Penelope had finally declared that she would marry whoever could best string Odysseus's great bow. None of the suitors could even bend the bow except, of course, for Odysseus who strung it, killed all the suitors and resumed his rightful place on the throne of Ithaca.

Transformations and Temptations

Europa and the Bull

It so happened that Europa, daughter of the king of Phoenicia, was out gathering flowers one day when Zeus saw her. Immediately, his heart was pierced with longing. To avoid the wrath of jealous Hera, he transformed himself into a beautiful bull and, standing next to Europa, he licked her neck while she stroked and kissed him. Indeed, the bull looked so inviting that Europa climbed onto his back whereupon the creature leapt into the air and sped away across the sea. The bull carried Europa to Crete and there the young girl had two sons by him: King Minos of Crete and King Rhadamanthys of the Cyclades.

Midas's Wish

One day, King Midas of Phrygia pleased Dionysus and so the god promised to grant him a wish. Without a moment's hesitation, Midas asked that whatever he touched might turn to gold. To test his new powers, the king broke off a twig from a tree; instantly, the twig turned to gold. He picked up a stone; that turned to gold too. The king was deliriously happy. Next, however, the king's servants set a meal before him. Midas picked up the bread; instantly, it turned to gold. The king mixed water and wine to drink; that turned to gold too. Eventually, starving and parched with thirst Midas cried out 'Father Dionysus, forgive me! Have pity!' Kindly Dionysus told Midas to wash himself in the source of the River Pactolus. The king did so and was cured immediately, but to this day the waters there run yellow with grains of gold.

The Ass's Ears

Out in the woods one day, Midas stumbled across a music contest between Pan and Apollo. Everyone thought Apollo's lyre sweeter than Pan's pipes – everyone, that is, except Midas. Outraged, Apollo inflicted Midas with an ass's ears. Midas tried to hide the ears beneath a purple turban but the servant who trimmed his hair saw them. Desperate to tell somebody, the servant whispered his secret into a hole in the earth. In due course, a clump of reeds grew from that very patch of soil and as the reeds rustled, they whispered to the wind the secret of the king's ears.

Echo and Narcissus

Echo was a nymph whose chatter so distracted
the goddess Hera that Zeus found plenty of
opportunity to have affairs. When Hera realized
what was happening, she took Echo's voice
away, allowing her merely to repeat the words of
others. Echo was in love with a beautiful youth
called Narcissus. She secretly followed him about,
unable to utter a single word. Eventually,
Narcissus called out: 'Is anyone here?'
whereupon Echo replied: 'Here!' Surprised,
Narcissus called out: 'Come to me!' whereupon
Echo replied: 'Me!' Irritated, Narcissus ran away
but Echo's love grew even stronger. Gradually,
she wasted away until only her voice remained.

The Death of Narcissus

In time, Narcissus's scornful attitude to love grew so irritating that the goddess Nemesis decided to punish him. One day, Narcissus lay down to drink at a fountain and fell madly in love with his own reflection. Countless times he tried to kiss himself, countless times he plunged his arms into the water seeking to embrace himself. Little by little, love wore him away until, at last, he died.

Daedalus and Icarus

When Minos discovered that Theseus had escaped from the Labyrinth, he was certain that Daedalus, its architect, must be responsible and so he threw him into prison, together with his son, Icarus. Undeterred, Daedalus constructed two vast pairs of wings and he and Icarus made their escape. Daedalus warned Icarus not to fly too close to the sun lest the glue on his wings should melt. However, Icarus soared up and up until his wings did indeed fall off and down into the sea he tumbled. The place where he fell became known as the Icarian Sea. Daedalus, meanwhile, flew on to Sicily.

Teiresias

One day, a young Theban called Teiresias came across two snakes mating. He killed the female snake whereupon he was immediately transformed into a young woman. For seven years Teiresias lived as a woman before finally resuming life as a man. Now, it so happened that Zeus and Hera were once caught up in a ferocious argument over whether men or women gained more pleasure from the act of love. They finally turned to Teiresias for advice. Teiresias took Zeus's side, saying that women gained more pleasure. Hera was furious and blinded Teiresias whereupon Zeus gave him the gift of second sight.

Io

One day, Zeus caught sight of Io, a beautiful priestess. When Io spurned his advances, Zeus trapped her in a fog and forced himself on her. Hera, suspicious of her husband, glided down to earth whereupon Zeus transformed Io into a cow. Io was still beautiful and so Hera claimed ownership of her, ordering the hundred-eyed Argus to guard her. On Zeus's command, Hermes killed Argus. Some say that Hera now became a gadfly and repeatedly stung Io. It was not until Io reached Egypt that she resumed her normal form. In due course she bore Zeus a child, Epaphus.

Callisto

Callisto liked nothing better than to hunt alongside the goddess Artemis in the fields of Arcadia. One day, Zeus saw the girl and, drawing close, he forced himself on her. In due course, Callisto gave birth to a son, Arcas. Zeus's wife, Hera, was furious and turned Callisto into a bear. Years later, when Arcas was out hunting, he came across the bear. Callisto tried to embrace her son but Arcas, terrified, tried to kill the beast. Just in time, Zeus snatched the bear away and placed her among the stars where she remains to this day as the constellation the Great Bear.

Athena and Arachne

There was once a gifted weaver, a peasant girl called Arachne, who claimed her work was even finer than Athena's. Outraged, Athena disguised herself as an old crone and warned the girl not to offend the gods. Arachne laughingly said she would love to pit her skills against Athena's. At this, the old crone assumed her real form and the two sat down to a weaving contest. Athena was forced to admire the girl's work but, furious at her impudence, she tore it into shreds. Arachne hanged herself whereupon the goddess turned her into a spider, condemned to weave beautiful webs for ever.

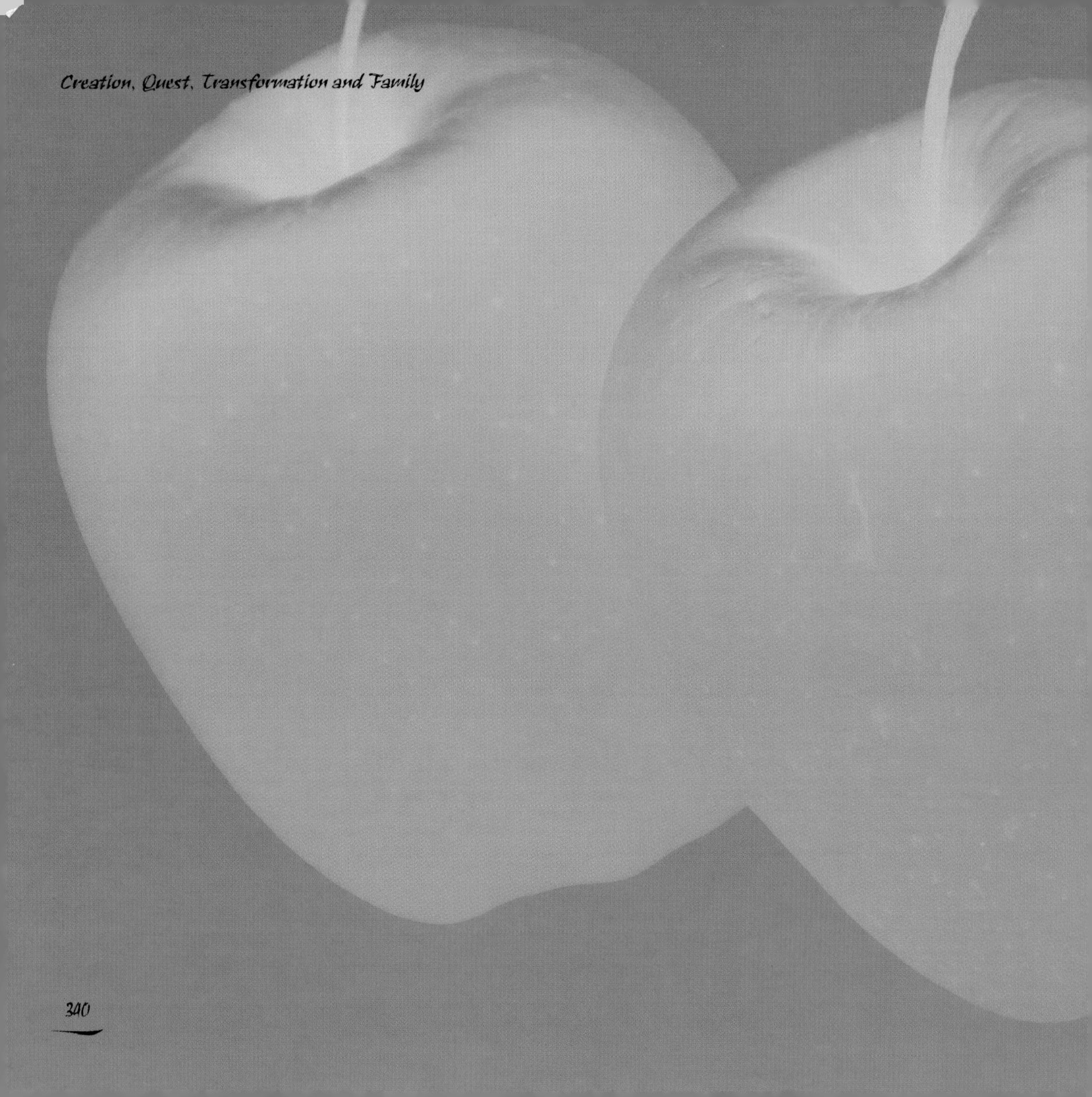

Atalanta

Atalanta's father was so distressed to have a daughter rather than a son that he left her on a hillside to die. The child was rescued by bears and raised by hunters. She became a great athlete and huntress, and she swore she would only marry a man who could outstrip her at running. Though many youths tried, none succeeded — until, that is, Hippomenes challenged her. During the race, Hippomenes rolled three fabulous golden apples in front of Atalanta, one at a time. Unable to resist stopping to pick them up, Atalanta lost the race and was forced to marry Hippomenes. Soon afterwards however, the couple offended Zeus by making love in one of his temples and he transformed them into lions.

Smyrna, Aphrodite and Adonis

Adonis was the product of an incestuous relationship between the King of Assyria and his daughter, Smyrna. The gods transformed Smyrna into a tree to save her from her father and it was from the trunk of this very tree that Adonis was born. Aphrodite was so struck with the child's beauty that she hid him away, giving him to Persephone to look after. Persephone, however, refused to return him. Zeus decided that Adonis should spend a third of each year with each goddess and the final third with whomsoever he chose. The youth always chose to spend two thirds of the year with Aphrodite. Out hunting one day, Adonis was gored to death by a boar. Aphrodite's grief knew no bounds.

Tantalus

Tantalus was the son of Zeus and a mortal woman. Although the gods were good to him, he talked too freely of divine affairs. Once, he even killed his son, Pelops, and served him to the gods as food. In punishment, Zeus sent Tantalus to Tartarus, the deepest realm of Hades, and suspended a huge rock above his head. Though Tantalus stood up to his neck in water, whenever he bent to drink, the water drained away. Above his head dangled bunches of delicious fruits but a gentle breeze blew them always just out of his reach.

Love, Marriage and Families

The Judgement of Paris

Eris, the goddess of discord, was furious at having been left off the guest-list for the wedding banquet of King Peleus and the nymph Thetis. Determined to cause trouble, she threw a golden apple into the banqueting hall; it was marked with the words 'For the Fairest'. All the goddesses wanted the apple but the competition was finally narrowed down to three: Aphrodite, Hera and Athena. Zeus ordered Paris, the son of King Priam of Troy, to judge the competition. The youth was amazed when the three goddesses appeared before him, and still more so by the bribes they offered him.

The Promises

Hera promised to make Paris ruler of Europe and Asia, Athena promised him great wisdom and victory in battle, Aphrodite promised him the most beautiful woman in the world. Paris gave the golden apple to Aphrodite. He abducted Helen, undoubtedly the most beautiful woman in the world, and for this reason the Trojan War was fought.

Eros and Psyche

There was once a king whose daughter, Pysche
('Soul'), was so beautiful that Aphrodite grew jealous of
her. The goddess told her son, Eros ('Love'), to pierce Psyche
with his arrow, hoping the girl would fall in love with a
disreputable wretch. That night, as Eros leant over Psyche, he
accidentally scratched himself and fell madly in love with her.
She, however, remained oblivious. The lovestruck Eros
persuaded Zeus to let Psyche be his whereupon Zephyr, the
west wind, swept the girl up to his magnificent palace.
Psyche could then only spend her nights with
Eros because she was forbidden
to see him.

The Jealous Sisters

Psyche's jealous sisters said her lover must be a horrible monster. That night,

Psyche lit a candle and looked at Eros; his beauty overwhelmed her. Eros,

however, was furious and stormed off. Devastated, Psyche begged Aphrodite for

help. The goddess ordered Psyche to perform several tasks which, against all odds,

she completed. Love and Soul were united at last.

Orpheus and Eurydice

Orpheus, the so-called father of song, was the son of a Muse and a Thracian king. He fell in love with and married Eurydice, either a woman or a nymph. One day, shortly after the marriage, Eurydice was running through a meadow when a snake bit her and she died. Heartbroken, Orpheus set out for the kingdom of Hades, determined to win her back. The moment he reached the underworld, Orpheus begged Hades and Persephone in song for the return of his beloved. So beautiful were the notes that tumbled from him that even the ghosts seemed to weep.

The Ascent

Hades and Persephone granted Orpheus his wish on condition that, during the ascent, he must not glance back at Eurydice one single time. If he did so, she must stay in the underworld for ever. The upwards path was dark and difficult and the air was thick with vapours. Just as they were emerging into the light, Orpheus cast a glance behind him. Instantly, Eurydice was pulled back into the depths. For seven whole days Orpheus paced the banks of the Styx weeping and grieving. At last, he gave up but for the rest of his life he refused to look at another woman.

The House of Mycenae

When Tantalus fed his son to the gods, they swore to punish his family for five generations. Tantalus was the grandfather of Atreus. When Atreus discovered that his wife was having an affair with his brother, Thyestes, he chopped Thyestes's two sons into pieces and cooked them, but for the hands and feet. Atreus then invited Thyestes to a feast, fed him his children and afterwards taunted him with the remaining pieces. Thyestes sought revenge. On the advice of an oracle, he fathered a child, Aegisthus, by his own daughter. When Aegisthus grew to manhood, he killed Atreus.

Agamemnon and Menelaus

Atreus was the father of Agamemnon and Menelaus.
Agamemnon married Clytemnestra and fathered two
children by her: Orestes and Electra. Meanwhile, Menelaus
married Helen. When Paris, Prince of Troy, abducted Helen,
the outrage sparked the Trojan War. Agamemnon led the
Greek forces to battle. In her husband's absence,
Clytemnestra took Aegisthus as her lover.

Matricide

Agamemnon finally returned from Troy bringing Cassandra with him as his concubine. Clytemnestra and Aegisthus killed both Agamemnon and Cassandra. Orestes, Agamemnon's son, was sent away while his daughter, Electra, remained at home. Years later, Orestes returned. He and Electra killed Aegisthus, then murdered their own mother.

Orestes and the Erinyes

Orestes was pursued by the
Erinyes to the brink of
insanity. Athena finally
decided that he should be
absolved of his crime.

The House of Thebes

Cadmus founded the city of Thebes. He married Harmonia and in due course his great grandson, Laius, became king. Laius married Jocasta; he also fell in love with and abducted to Thebes a boy called Chrysippos, the illegitimate son of Pelops. It was this transgression that sparked off all the terrible events that followed.

The Family of Cadmus and Oedipus

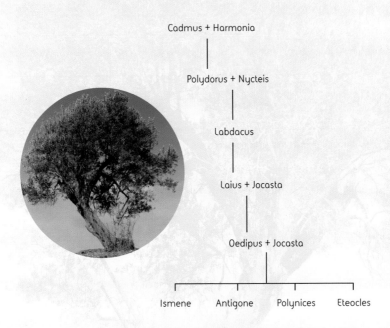

Cadmus + Harmonia

|

Polydorus + Nycteis

|

Labdacus

|

Laius + Jocasta

|

Oedipus + Jocasta

Ismene   Antigone   Polynices   Eteocles

The Birth of Oedipus

The Delphic oracle warned Laius and Jocasta that they would have a child who killed his father. Nonetheless, when Laius was drunk one night, the couple conceived Oedipus. As soon as the baby was born, they had him exposed on a mountainside. However, the baby was rescued and raised by the king of Corinth. Years later, Oedipus consulted the Delphic oracle and was told that he would kill his own father and lie with his mother. Thinking his parents were the king and queen of Corinth, Oedipus determined never to return there.

The Oracle is Fulfilled

On the road from Delphi, Oedipus met an old man
who refused to let him pass by. Not realizing that
this was Laius, his true father, Oedipus killed him.
Next, hearing that the neighbouring city of Thebes
was being plagued by the monstrous Sphinx,
Oedipus hurried to help out. The Sphinx challenged
all passers-by to answer her riddle or die. Oedipus
solved the riddle whereupon the Sphinx threw
herself to her death. Oedipus's reward was to
marry Jocasta. Mother and son had a fruitful
marriage: two sons, Eteocles and Polynices and
two daughters, Antigone and Ismene.

The Discovery

Time passed, and Thebes was struck by a terrible plague. Determined to uncover its cause, Oedipus found, to his horror, that he was to blame. After speaking to the herdsman who had exposed him on the mountain, he realized that Laius and Jocasta were his parents and that, as the oracle had predicted, he had murdered his father and married his mother. It was these monstrous acts that had blighted Thebes. Jocasta, in her shame, committed suicide but Oedipus, unable to face meeting his parents in the underworld, blinded himself.

The Riddle of the Sphinx

What goes on four legs in the morning, on two legs at noon, and on three legs in the evening?

Answer: Man — we are on four legs as a baby, two legs as an adult, and walk with a cane in old age.

Creation, Quest, Transformation and Family

The House of Athens

Pandion, King of Athens, married his daughter, Procne, to Tereus, King of Thrace. The couple had a son, Itys. Tereus lusted after Procne's sister, Philomela, and forced himself on her. Afterwards, he cut out Philomela's tongue so she could not speak of the crime. However, Philomela wove a marvellous tapestry which showed Procne all that had passed. In revenge, Procne killed Itys and fed him to Tereus. Then she and Philomela made their escape. Tereus caught up with the sisters and was about to kill them when the gods transformed them all into birds. Philomela became the swallow, Procne the nightingale and Tereus the hoopoe.

'Old myths, old gods, old heroes have never died.

They are only sleeping at the bottom of our mind,

waiting for our call. We have need for them.

They represent the wisdom of our race.'

Stanley Kunitz (1905–2006)